Cybersecurity Evolved

5 Principles to Stay
Ahead of the Game

RANDY LINDBERG

Contents

Contents

1
Beginnings

In 1999 the US Air Force sent me to a 2,500-person software development facility in Montgomery, Alabama where I was slotted to be the Information Systems Security Officer.

Given that cybersecurity wasn't on many people's radar back then, this was new territory for me and I wasn't so sure my Management Information Systems degree and previous experience working on network projects really equipped me for the role. As I recall, in the end, much of my job entailed keeping a 3-inch binder of technical diagrams, IT asset lists, firewall rules, and basic security controls up-to-date and reporting to the base commander every quarter.

Looking back, this all seems very low-key, given that even then organized crime was already starting to pose a threat online, a threat that's grown way, way bigger ever since, and one that's pulled cybersecurity along in its wake. Even, by 2008, the US government was talking about spending $17 billion on a cybersecurity initiative.

Cybersecurity is now a global industry, of course, where our success tends to be measured by the 'absence' of anything happening. So, every breach that makes a headline is marked down as a failure.

If you like, we are the equivalent of the doormen at a nightclub who try to stop the wrong people from getting in but can't be sure a fight won't happen sometime at the bar.

But if our job is protecting organizations from the bad guys then some people might say it's a job we're not particularly good at it given a whole bunch of statistics out there that make for grim reading.

Ransomware, payment fraud, corporate espionage, intellectual property theft, and disinformation campaigns are all rising at an alarming rate. In 2021, for instance, the FBI's Internet Crime Complaint Center said it received a record 847,376 complaints with a combined potential loss of nearly $7 billion. That same year, losses from cybercrime damages were put at around $6 trillion[1] with the financial losses from it calculated at around $190,000 per second. Put all this together and cybercrimes are costing the equivalent of about 0.8% of the world's GDP[2]. And things are not showing any signs of improvement, in fact, quite the reverse.

In 2022, ransomware attacks on companies were looking to be a third higher[3] than they were the previous year. And this is a criminal activity that just keeps on taking, with many companies having paid up once to get their systems back and then finding themselves being attacked once again by the same perpetrators.

Disappointingly, whatever the flavor of this organized threat, there's little chance anyone will be caught for their cyber sins. In the US, for instance, the likelihood of detecting and prosecuting the perpetrators of cyberattacks was put at a dismal 0.05% by the World Economic Forum in 2020.[4]

Of course, not long ago, you might have been able to console yourself that this was something that only happened to big business, those in particular sectors like finance, or with high-value clients. But that's no longer the case. Cyber threats are no longer confined to particular sectors. This is something that can happen to any organization, anytime, anywhere — over half of all cyberattacks are now aimed at small- to medium-sized enterprises.

And with about one in six (16%) organizations receiving over 100,000 security alerts every day according to Cisco, unless you are lucky or have in place a sufficiently robust resilience plan, on the wrong day a malicious cyber event could see the end of your business — six out of ten SMBs that are hacked or suffer a data breach fold within just six months.[5] This is the modern equivalent of a fire that 30 years ago would have brought a business down because it destroyed all the paperwork in your filing cabinets.

It all seems rather prescient of Warren Buffet, the billionaire investor, who back in 2017 called cybercrime the number one problem for mankind[6] and I suspect nothing's happened to change his mind since.

So, not only do we have organized crime gangs launching attacks but there are also state-sponsored operators. North Korea, for instance, has a history of stealing cryptocurrencies as part of its strategy for dealing with the country's financial isolation. Crypto-research firm Chainalysis calculated that in the first half of 2022, the regime stole over $840 million.

And things are only going to get worse. Cybercriminals are becoming ever more sophisticated as they begin to use artificial intelligence, for instance, to increase the volume of their attacks. And if you've been paying attention to the Industrial Internet of Things (IIoT) you know it's going to dramatically increase the number of devices going online and that's going to exponentially expand the potential attack surface. In 2019, the number of hits on IoT devices rose by 300% according to the World Economic Forum and that number is going to get bigger when 5G telecoms — the primary communications network for connected devices — get rolled out even further. That wouldn't be so bad perhaps if IoT vendors were better at meeting security standards, but sadly, they're notorious for not doing so.

And if these maligned external threats weren't enough, then we also have the everyday data breaches that are caused by error, incompetence, and inefficiency in a company's internal systems.

Given all this, some security leaders, perhaps not surprisingly, are saying we are heading into an era of increased risk. So, I don't think the significance of cybersecurity can be overstated.

Corporate complacency still rules

And unfortunately, by the nature of the game, inevitably we're always playing catch up. Because of the impossibility of anticipating an attacker's every move, we're always at least one step behind the bad actors. But you probably don't need me saying that we are in a kind of arms race with the bad guys and they are winning. All we can do is keep trying to react faster to make things as difficult as possible for them.

The introduction of dozens of laws and regulations over the last 20 years or so, has undoubtedly slowed the online threat to some extent by forcing organizations to focus more on their cybersecurity and giving them some practical frameworks for doing so — NIST, ISO 27001/02,

SOC2, NERC-CIP, HIPAA, GDPR and FISMA and the like. But despite this legislative muscle, we're still a long way from where we need to be.

As an industry, we are faced with a further problem, which is that security is still viewed by many business leaders, and a significant proportion of those in IT, not as a strategic investment that can save a company a significant amount of money, which it is, but rather as a cost sink draining money away from where it could be better spent. In some ways, this is the same attitude we have toward household insurance which we pay out every month and which feels like a pointless and unnecessary expense until our home gets flooded or hit by a tornado!

This means in many cases cybersecurity remains just an afterthought, which is why you frequently find many companies doing the very bare minimum to comply with regulations. So, though lots of organizations may *say* they recognize the importance of cybersecurity, they never make addressing potential cyber threats a strategic priority.

This means that all too often, you have a mismatch between the *real* degree of risk from cyberattacks and the degree of threat *perceived* by business leaders which is what affects their decision-making and resource allocation.

This kind of laissez-faire attitude is found right through many organizations and often among those who should know better. CISOs, for instance, are often looked down upon by CIOs because they are thought to get in the way of the everyday management of an organization's tech infrastructure. In effect, they are seen as the equivalent of an overly-cautious Health and Safety Officer who is always telling everyone what they can't do because it's too dangerous. More than once at a large corporation I've had someone senior in IT tell me "do what you have to do but stay out of my way."

This was certainly the attitude I experienced as a contractor when configuring a security information and event management (SEIM) solution for a power company where the IT leadership team had been in place for over 15 years. Of course, there's nothing inherently wrong with having the same leaders in place for a long time, but there is when they never allow themselves to be influenced by fresh ideas and new ways of thinking.

Unfortunately, over a decade and a half, everyone in this team had developed not just a collective groupthink about the problems they faced but also false and unfounded confidence in their own abilities to solve them. So, any suggestion from a new employee, or an outsider like me, was given no weight and quickly disregarded.

And because they all thought the same way, no one ever considered how things could be made better, and no improvements were ever made. As a result, the department was poorly run, underpinned by inadequate, out-of-date IT, and riddled with generally poor security practices.

This kind of situation is typical in businesses that don't take cybersecurity seriously.

But no organization can keep sitting on its hands and not doing what needs to be done indefinitely.

In some situations, security teams are coming under pressure from their cyber insurance companies demanding that highly specific and ever more onerous security controls are put in place before they will consider issuing a cyber policy. Recently, one of our clients returned from sick leave to find a list of 20 'security demands' from their insurer that needed to be complied with. Not the sort of thing you want to come back to when you've been ill.

When they phoned us for help, I could hear the anxiety in his voice. I could tell he thought this was going to be a major project that would entail monumental effort, cost lots of money, and take up weeks of his time. And I guess if he'd been trying to resolve everything on his own, or even with a team, then it would.

Fortunately, using our software platform and processes we were able to map out all the insurance company's requirements in just a few minutes so he was able to identify and provide evidence for the 20 controls that were needed very quickly. Anxiety attack over.

Who is this book for?

Undoubtedly, our job as cybersecurity professionals is getting harder and harder, and that means we need to take a long hard look at the way we do things.

And in large part, this is why I've written this book because over the years I've been able to observe how we as an industry go about our business and it's felt as though something isn't quite right. To me, there seems to be far too large a gap between the technical operations side of cybersecurity and the business side of an organization. These are two halves that really do need to work together and understand each other, but rarely do.

So, this short book is for you if you sit on the management side of the cybersecurity fence — one of the Chief Information Security Officers (CISOs), Virtual Chief Information Security Officers (vCISOs), or other security professionals who have to deal with all the stuff that gets thrown at them when there's an audit finding or actual cyber-attack. And I hope it will go some way to equipping you as a cybersecurity manager with a better understanding of how you can make cybersecurity part of your business systems and processes — the kind of stuff that sits between the technical side of cybersecurity and the business.

Who am I to tell you what to do?

But this isn't a book that's going to send you down some technological rabbit hole. In fact, I've written it for those on the management side of cybersecurity — the managers who must deal with the recriminations that come their way when there is a successful cyber-attack.

This brings us to the point where you might be asking, who am I to be providing new ways of thinking about cybersecurity management? In other words, why believe what I'm saying?

And that's a fair question.

My answer is that after working nearly a quarter of a century in cybersecurity I've been considering the issues for a long time.

In some circles I describe myself as an amateur futurist — that means I like thinking about how the world may play out and, how technology, is going to impact our lives for both good and bad.

I also declare myself a cybersecurity geek. And you can tell how much when I rather sheepishly reveal that *NIST 800-30 Risk Management* was essential bedtime reading for me when it was first published in 2002. In fact, I built a PMP-style process around it, that was subsequently used to perform the first-ever state-wide risk assessment for the State of Florida and the 30-plus agencies it had at the time.

And now having worked with a wide range of leading companies, especially in the finance sector, I've reached a point where I'm confident I have something to say based on the knowledge and experience I've gained over the years.

Back in 2010, I founded Rivial Data Security, with the explicit aim of making cybersecurity management that much easier for businesses.

The firm's original slogan, "Cybersecurity is not a trivial matter, but managing it should be", was a little cheesy but reflected the approach I still take today — doing the best job possible in the simplest possible way.

Rivial Data Security (Rivial, by the way, is 'Trivial' without the 'T') allowed me to get up close and personal with many different companies, which gave me a strong understanding of their needs and, in particular, how they weren't being best served by traditional cybersecurity management software.

After a few years of listening and reinventing cybersecurity management processes, the firm morphed into the cybersecurity firm it is today, with the Rivial Platform, which I'll talk more about later, emerging from it.

But, enough of the history lesson. Let's look at what is currently wrong with cybersecurity management.

2
Vanity Metrics Are Not Enough

I've heard it said that cybersecurity can be likened to the brakes on a car. Because we have them, we can go faster since we know we can slow down. Without brakes, we'd get places much slower because we'd be worried about crashing.

So, what's the lesson to be learned here? Simple. Don't think of security as an additional cost or something that slows progress because it's actually the opposite.

But many businesses still don't see it that way. As a security professional you know cybersecurity isn't being taken as seriously as it should be in a lot of organizations.

Part of the blame for this situation lies with us cybersecurity professionals who continue to fail to make the case for its importance.

This means that for all the good work the cybersecurity industry does, it is continually compromised by an inability to establish its strategic credentials.

Instead of finding themselves with their feet under the executive table, cybersecurity professionals are often regarded as offering nothing more than a tactical tool that sits firmly within the realm of IT.

But why is that when it is a very real and present danger to their existence?

In many cases, the simple reason is that business leaders do not fully understand how to make decisions about the threats they face, so they choose to ignore them.

And why don't they understand the significance of this cyber threat? Well, I think there are a few factors at play here, the first of which is the invisibility of our 'product'.

If you take a technical sport like motor racing or road cycling, you can see how cars and bikes have evolved. You look at them and see that by building on what's gone before, the latest iterations are better and faster.

But cybersecurity isn't like that. You can't easily see what security controls are like or understand how much better they've become unless you are one of the few people who know how to spot the 'sexy security architecture' that's gone into it. So, any improvements are invisible.

On top of this, cybersecurity tends to be considered a complex topic that is too difficult to understand unless you come from a technical background. And because it is considered a complex subject, it is also assumed that complex solutions are needed to solve it.

Consequently, business leaders either make little attempt to learn about it or take an almost fatalistic approach of 'what happens will happen.'

Now I know many of you will be shouting, "but cybersecurity management is difficult. It is hard, and that's just the way it is."

Well, let me respectfully disagree and say that if we continue to act as though managing cybersecurity is impossibly hard, we will be doing nothing to encourage better cybersecurity and that will leave many organizations insufficiently protected against the risk of an attack.

Cybersecurity isn't as hard as we make it out to be, and if we hide some of the 'difficult stuff under the rug' by automating a lot of the hard grind, we can make it easier still.

Of course, as an industry, it should be our duty to ensure that business leaders do understand the importance of cybersecurity so they can make the best and most rational strategic decisions, and this must be based on information from others that is timely and relevant.

Unfortunately, this is a task at which we have largely failed simply because we have failed to communicate to those at the top of organizations what could be done.

So, while a security professional may get excited about the mechanics of a particular SQL Injection Attack or Cross-Site Scripting, to most people in an organization, this is just gobbledygook. We are strange beasts that talk an unknown and undecipherable language known only to a few.

By talking in jargonized language, consultants reassure themselves and justify to others that they are 'the experts' who justify their big bucks, but in reality, this does nothing when it comes to creating the understanding necessary among business leaders.

One of the main arguments of this book is that security professionals need to make much greater efforts to ensure cybersecurity isn't perceived as 'difficult.'

If business leaders can't follow what you are saying or continually have to ask for clarification, then you have lost the battle for understanding. It also means those who need to be making well-thought-through strategic decisions will find it difficult, if not impossible, to do so because they don't fully appreciate the significance of what is presented to them in a cybersecurity status report.

This makes us the messengers who cannot put our message across — the professionals who are supposedly there to keep the Board up to date about threats and vulnerabilities but then struggle to convey what is going on.

And when there is this lack of understanding, inevitably, you don't get the creation or build-up of trust that's necessary for business leaders to make the right decisions. As has been said: It's the ability to stop quickly that allows us to travel fast. Without brakes, we would all be driving very slowly[7.] And it's this message we must work hard to put across.

Poor communication

So, rather than wrapping the security message up in technical jargon and vanity metrics, we need to speak in the language of the C-suite and board members of the companies that hire them.

Bridging this 'messaging gap' is something we've always sought to address at Rivial by making effective, relevant communication central to what we do.

And so, we do what we can to help our clients communicate their message more effectively. For example, we were working recently with a CISO who was continually frustrated by the Board, who never gave any credence to her recommendations. Anything she proposed that cost more than a few hundred dollars was quickly shot down in flames.

But after performing a thorough risk assessment and some strategic planning, we could chop $200,000 out of her proposed budget without limiting the real risk reduction of the cybersecurity program. And because these were based on ROI, the board got a real sense of the benefit to the business. And that was the moment that a more trusting relationship began to build. By applying the principles and new presentation method we gave her, she can now push through ever more complex solutions because the Board appreciates the business logic behind them. So, even strong resistance to cybersecurity by business leaders can be overcome with an effective communications approach.

And since cybersecurity is not just a leadership matter but everyone's issue, all stakeholders in the organization must better understand cybersecurity's importance and how they can play their part in managing risk.

There must be channels through which employees can communicate their concerns and lower, middle, and upper management should be open to communicating about risks with employees because they see different things at varying levels within the company. They should be encouraged to bring their concerns forward so they can properly be investigated.

More than one way TO DO things

Over the years, it has become clearer that while the cybersecurity industry may not yet be completely broken, the way we manage it surely is.

Though some things work and are undoubtedly better than they were, there is still much room for improvement.

To put it bluntly, cybersecurity professionals need to get better at what we do and provide greater value to the business. As it is, there are just too many firms charging big bucks for what is, at best, a mediocre service overseen by disinterested auditors who appear once a year to perform a tick-box exercise in compliance, before disappearing for another year without providing any guidance or help with the shortcomings their inspection may have revealed.

Is this good enough? I don't think so.

In my mind, the cybersecurity management industry needs to reinvent itself. Rather than getting bogged down focusing on a plethora of controls, we should concentrate instead on the big picture, and what I have set out in this book is an alternative approach based on five core principles.

Collectively, we've dug ourselves into a hole, thinking more about the technicalities of what we do rather than focusing on the outcomes we're meant to deliver for our clients. In other words, most cybersecurity professionals have been using crummy processes for so long, they don't recognize there's a different way of doing things.

Keeping on 'doing things the way they've always been done' is one of those attitudes that's always bugged me. I guess that's because if you want to define me, I'm that annoying guy in the corner who's always asking, "why?"

And it's only when you ask yourself, "is there a better way of doing this?" that innovation occurs.

For me, coming up with innovative ideas on securing a business is enjoyable and almost a matter of pride. If I'm not doing that, then it just feels wrong.

And it was this process that ultimately led to the development of the next generation of managing a cybersecurity program.

I tried and used NIST 800-30, Octave, and even Microsoft's monstrous risks assessment spreadsheet (circa 2004, anybody remember that thing?) because they seemed useful. But the more I used them, the more I came across serious flaws and issues that increasingly frustrated me and the executives I was reporting to. And because I didn't see any good reason for perpetuating a sub-optimal way of working if we didn't have to, I decided to build my own risk assessment methodology.

Our risk management model has a highly defined structure, but with inherent flexibility, so users can modify different components to reflect inputs such as information type, risk indicators, and the number of times a simulation has been run around a specific incident or event.

I must admit to being a bit biased, but I believe our way of doing things is right at the front of the market because it is so streamlined, yet very comprehensive and adds a ton of value that's beyond people's expectations.

One CISO client, a very smart guy with over 20 years in IT and cybersecurity, knows what he's doing. The day I walked him through the way Rivial approaches cybersecurity management, it was a revelation for him. It changed the way he thinks about cybersecurity.

I like to break cybersecurity into two main parts: technical and management. Security Orchestration Automation & Response (SOAR) (or whatever the term du jour is this quarter) is the technology bundle that collects, analyses, and responds to inputs from all different pieces of security being monitored by an organization.

And although SOAR provides a useful framework for identifying and responding to attacks, it focuses on the operational aspect of cybersecurity rather than its management. It runs beneath the cybersecurity management function.

Though the technology is there to make cybersecurity operations more seamless and responsive, it does nothing to integrate the fragmented nature of security management. Take a look at the pieces going into most organizations' cybersecurity programs, and you'll have a list that runs something like this:

- IT Risk Assessments
- IT Audits
- Vulnerability Assessments
- Vendor Assessments
- Penetration Testing
- Incident Response
- User Training
- Social Engineering

That's messy, right?

And we all know how this translates into day-to-day reality, piles of printed documents, spreadsheets, screenshots, and scattered IT audit reports and risk assessments all containing rarely connected information.

This means capturing all the ripples arising from any action in this complex ecosystem is time-consuming and just about impossible using spreadsheets. And don't think that will even be nearly 100% accurate.

3
Fighting Back

This creates a gap between how cybersecurity should be managed and how it is. And this is a gap that must be closed if we are to ensure executives trust us and the organization is as protected as possible.

And to do that, we came up with a new approach that enables organizations to improve their security in a far more holistic and effective way. It's based on a framework of five core principles that we have developed over the years, working to make cybersecurity management much easier to the point it becomes almost trivial.

When implemented successfully, the principles reduce the burden of cybersecurity management through automation and the de-duplication of effort when you're trying to comply with multiple security control frameworks.

We used this core concept to create the Rivial Platform[8], the world's most integrated and automated cybersecurity management software, when it launched in early 2022. This software works across all functions of the security program and has the flexibility to continuously recognize what impact a change in one area might have upon another. It also gives users the ability to capture all the ripples arising from any one action, so it's easy to see how just one piece of evidence affects both your compliance standing, risk ratings, and executive reporting.

The five principles add a new level of sophistication to your information security program that will improve how you look at cybersecurity. More importantly, they will change how your stakeholders look at your cybersecurity program.

I must admit that developing the Rivial Platform hadn't been our original plan, which was to create a cyber risk quantification tool as an add-on to one of our business partner's products.

But as they say, 'it grew in the telling' as we kept building more functionality. Eventually, we ended up with a comprehensive solution covering all major components of managing cybersecurity programs — risk, compliance, vendor cybersecurity management, vulnerability management, incident response planning, and all the external security tools and technologies that go with this.

And having seen us use it, our clients started asking to buy the software, and from there, we went on to work with channel partners that have introduced the platform to more and more.

Of course, you don't need to use the Rivial Platform to create the holistic viewpoint we're discussing here. You could, for instance. create your own digital hub using code, spreadsheets, and SharePoint. Later in this book, I will discuss each of the five principles and provide basic steps to implement each step on your own with free or existing tools you probably already have.

Or you could build your own software. While this may be a good long-term plan, I can tell you from experience that it's the high-risk path and one that's hard to get right.

I know a vCISO who spent years cobbling together a solution from a combination of GRC tools. It worked ... up to a point, but he absolutely hated using it, which is why he now uses our software to update his clients' cybersecurity programs automatically.

And I certainly wouldn't recommend the balancing act of operating a growing a consulting company while simultaneously being a software start-up. This is how we built the Rivial Platform, and I have a lot more grey hair as a result. We put every available dollar into building the platform. And although I proudly park my Toyota pickup among the BMW's of my business owner peers, I know we built something great. But I wouldn't do it again, knowing how low the odds of success are creating new software!

Reinventing what's broken

I'm writing this book right now because I think the cybersecurity sector is facing an approaching storm that will mean it is even less well-equipped to deal with the threats we're facing.

It would be great to think that the cybersecurity sector is going to become ever more effective and that, somehow, we will begin to gain some traction so we can beat back the threat that's coming towards. I wish that were true. But I can see quite the opposite happening.

I think we are now at an inflection point in cybersecurity, heading towards a perfect storm that will necessitate a rapid and significant shift in how cybersecurity is managed.

This storm is being created by twin forces, a massive talent shortage, and the second I've already talked about — the increase in hacking and cyberattacks. Remember those statistics from earlier?

Ransomware attacks are particularly prevalent,[9] with around two-thirds of cybersecurity leaders saying they'd experienced one in the last year.

And this constant barrage of attacks is not just causing concern, it is also having a major impact on the security professionals trying to repel them. This is the second part of the storm.

For many cybersecurity professionals, the inability of their organizations to hire suitable talent means that not only are heavier workloads being imposed on them but they are also expected to take on roles and tasks that are out of their comfort zone.

With increased cyber threats creating new risks for businesses, this is heaping on additional pressure reflected in high levels of stress and burnout. As a result, many are leaving the profession through sickness or choosing to resign from their roles. One global study found that about a third are considering leaving their current position[10] over the next two years because of stress and burnout.

This all adds up to a growing shortage of suitably qualified professionals to deliver the cybersecurity management functions needed. This massive talent shortage is reflected in the millions of unfilled security jobs worldwide. Many warned of this potential problem five years ago, but unfortunately, little was done to address it.

And this global talent shortage is occurring at just the moment when more people are required to deal with the increased demand for their services. It's a vicious circle that's hard to break.

The time to fix cybersecurity management is now. Before, it gets significantly worse for all of us. By implementing the five principles in this book, you can fix cybersecurity management at your organization.

4

The 5 Principles

Given this backdrop, the only realistic option for many organizations is to look for a technology solution since there's no other way for them to get the resources they need to keep up.

Unfortunately, much of the technology being used right now for cybersecurity management is based on decades old principles. Very often, the software used just isn't sophisticated enough to do what needs to be done. At worst, we are talking about little more than a glorified online spreadsheet, and no matter how detailed it is, trying to manage your risk and compliance with a spreadsheet hasn't been realistic since the early 2000s.

But coming up with a viable alternative means approaching this issue from a more holistic direction.

As it stands currently, the standard cybersecurity process feels highly fragmented, probably because the environment we operate is very much driven by compliance. In other words, we focus on meeting externally determined criteria created by regulators to achieve a benchmark standard in different areas.

But these elements aren't separate. They are all part of the same ecosystem, and you can't see that properly when they have been treated individually for more than 20 years.

Slicing and dicing services in this way just reinforces the impression that cybersecurity management consists of a collection of separated components for handling strategy, risk, compliance, vendor security assessment, vulnerability management, incident response planning, and executive reporting when cybersecurity management programs should be seen as something seamless and holistic.

This kind of thinking is also reflected in how security consulting is offered, with organizations having to choose from a menu of separate services.

And because compliance has become the driving force behind cybersecurity, the belief has grown almost subconsciously that being compliant is all about being able to check all the boxes. Achieve that, and it's a job well done. While that might sound fine in theory, Im sure we all know this isn't true.

And as the list of security control frameworks grows, so does the number of boxes we have to check. This can lead to a sense of overwhelm which can almost create paralysis and uncertainty, which isn't a good place to be. No wonder so many professionals are leaving the industry.

On top of this, the frustration comes from knowing that many of these different controls require the same or highly similar information. That means that to complete them, you are duplicating so much effort in both transferring data and tweaking it to meet slightly different needs.

For a CISO or vCISO cheking all the boxes is a bit like doing your regular shopping at the supermarket using a separate ingredient list for every recipe that week. If you follow each list to the letter, then you'll find yourself with far more ingredients than you need, and that's going to cost you time and money. This is why it's so much more efficient to sit down and work out how to share ingredients across recipes, so you pick up only what's needed as you go through the aisles.

Why not do the same with cybersecurity management? If we were to concentrate on outcomes rather than the wording of individual controls, we could simplify and integrate all those security checklists.

But that requires us to start thinking of cybersecurity as being much more of an ecosystem of functions. And it's such a high-level thought that's been central to what we do at Rivial and how we do it.

In developing the Rivial Platform, we wanted to help cybersecurity professionals deliver greater value to organizations by creating a single tool that integrated multiple functions. In other words, it would interconnect functions that have traditionally been treated separately.

I'm pleased to say our approach works.

One of our HIPAA consulting partners described the Rivial Platform as "way more mature" than anything else available in the market. While one of our financial services clients was told by an examiner that "no one else was doing what we were doing because it's so cutting edge."

And another client has been able to achieve the highest rating possible from an IT examiner, who had previously told her that getting such a score was "impossible."

We are quickly building a reputation as a firm that has solved an unsolvable problem. This is great to hear and validates our approach, at the heart of which are five principles you can apply by creating your own system or using the Rivial Platform. Either way, I hope you'll join us on the journey to the next evolution of cybersecurity management and help fix an entire industry along the way.

In the next section, I'll describe each of the five principles and set out how you can apply them as part of your security program with or without the Rivial Platform.

Principle 1
A Single Pane of Glass

The Problem

Traditionally, cybersecurity management is a list of disconnected functions involving individual standalone tools or spreadsheets that cannot connect with one another. Having to switch between multiple tools, documents, and screens to deal with different functions is a scenario cybersecurity professionals know only too well. That's inefficient and wastes time, as anyone responsible for a cybersecurity program will know.

Not only is this disconnectedness inconvenient, it also means data and functionality become siloed in different parts of an organization. In terms of cybersecurity, this can leave CISOs with a fragmented and incomplete picture of where risks lie.

And because these different applications don't mesh together, sharing information between them is hard. Data must be frequently entered and re-entered into different applications, so it takes time to stitch together details from various applications and then make sense of it all.

This means there's much duplication of effort and a greater chance that something will fall between the cracks and be missed.

The Solution

However, life gets a lot easier when you start thinking about program management, risk, compliance, IR planning, and vendor security reviews as parts of the same function.

The ideal method is to gather all this information together and then present what matters most on a 'single pane of glass' where the data from different cybersecurity functions is gathered side-by-side in a single unified view. Life suddenly gets a great deal easier. You get a complete picture of the security program and can make faster, better decisions.

Imagine if you had a system that automatically creates a Jira ticket and sends you a Slack message because it recognized a vulnerability management automated KPI had not been met, and the risk had risen beyond a dollar threshold. Then this would be the kind of detailed information any CISO/vCISO could act on with confidence.

The DIY Option

1. Log into each security tool you are using.

2. Pull key details from each into a database or spreadsheet.

3. Cross-check that these details are correct.

4. Set key performance indicators for each line item in the database or spreadsheet you have set up.

5. Plug in details from each function and tool. Do this periodically.

6. Create your dashboard, the single pane of glass where you can see your cybersecurity program in one place.

7. This dashboard should pull together data about risk, compliance and policy management, evidence gathering, incident response planning and exercising, vulnerability management, and vendor cybersecurity assessment.

8. You now have a system for better, more confident decision-making about your security program.

The Rivial Platform Approach

And that's exactly what the Rivial Platform does by creating what is, in effect, a 'dashboard of dashboards.'

No more having to log into three or four different tools to download all the information needed to collate a monthly status report for the Board, as many cybersecurity professionals must do.

The platform also ensures information that is entered into one part of the system automatically flows to other areas where it was needed. Again, no more having to inefficiently copy and paste data from one place to another.

Think of all the time you could then spend doing things that are more strategic and more important.

And because data is being seamlessly channelled to where it's needed, nothing falls between the cracks and gets lost, since everything is in plain sight.

When you have a granular view like this, you can tailor controls to the compliance requirements to see how this changes the organization's risk profile. Unsure if you will remain within tolerance if you vary a control slightly? The system will tell you. This means that you can effectively do 'what-if' analyses for different actions to make systems get tighter and more streamlined over time. That leads to ever-better decision-making.

Principle 2
Focus on Jobs to be Done

The Problem

Achieving compliance is the ever-present backdrop for any cybersecurity management system, with anything that alters your security profile being a variable that will toggle you from compliance to non-compliance and back again.

So, checking the boxes of a security control framework is often seen as the primary goal of cybersecurity. And if you are following multiple frameworks, this can entail having to check a lot of boxes. For something as 'simple' as antivirus, this could mean confirming 5, 10, or 15 times that the appropriate AV controls are in place.

The traditional approach has been control 'crosswalks' and matrices of controls that make a feeble attempt at coordinating multiple control frameworks. I won't mention names, but you can even spend $5-10k on a control framework that maps to all frameworks. One framework to rule them all, if you will.

In practice, this line of thinking is backward. Adding another control framework to fix the problem of too many control frameworks is not logical. And in reality, it means that to cover all the bases, you will still have to generate three or four 'sub-reports' from different apps that must be collated to create a single master presentation to the Board.

The Solution

We started to ask ourselves: rather than always focusing on the individual wording of each control framework, is there a way to help cybersecurity professionals focus more on their primary overarching outcome — making an organization safe and secure?

The solution to the problem of too many security control frameworks is not to add another framework or crosswalk multiple lists of controls. The solution is to ignore the control frameworks, at least temporarily, and focus on the security jobs that need doing.

If somebody is responsible for antivirus, their job is to ensure agents are deployed and reporting regularly, signatures are kept up to date, and the right KPIs are met. The evidence of this job being done is a report from the antivirus management console demonstrating that these items are in place.

The person doing the job of antivirus doesn't need to know they are complying with PCI DSS requirement 5, CIS Critical Security Control 10, and ACET Domain 3 Item 190. They need to know what is expected of them, how to produce the evidence, and where and when to provide it.

Keep it simple and focus on the jobs to be done. An evidence list of about 120 items can comply with hundreds of individual controls across multiple frameworks. Mapping evidence to controls can be done once, on the backend, where nobody needs to worry about it. No framework to rule all frameworks necessary.

The DIY Option

1. Identify the evidence needed to demonstrate security jobs being done.

2. Map evidence to controls and check for overlap. If you comply with 400-500 or more controls across varying frameworks, you might end up with only 80-100 evidence items.

3. Schedule timelines for collecting evidence items.

4. Allocate responsibility for generating evidence to an appropriate individual or team.

5. Create a common cybersecurity calendar with automated reminders based on the agreed collection schedule.

6. Prompt those collecting evidence to upload it an appropriate time.

7. Provide a link to SharePoint or an internal shared drive where evidence can be uploaded for centralized tracking.

The Rivial Platform Approach

With the Rivial Platform, we link controls from various frameworks to a single set of evidence. Based on a flexible schedule, the platform notifies evidence owners when an item is about to expire. Once evidence is uploaded from all your different security functions, the software does all the hard work of running through the different checklists of all control frameworks and highlights any areas of non-compliance.

This means that regardless of the control framework. Each evidence is checked against requirements, and the system is automatically updated. This is done for both risk assessment and compliance controls. The latest tracking and cybersecurity reports can then be quickly generated for the management team. This means you can focus on what needs to be done — any unchecked boxes.

Principle 3
Real-Time Updates

The Problem

In the realm of cybersecurity, once-yearly risk assessments and compliance audits are the norm. But how does this traditional approach stack up when technology environments are continually changing and doing so faster than ever?

The answer is ... it doesn't. And just as with dental appointments, a lot can happen between visits.

Today, for instance, you might have a control that's operating fine, but then doesn't tomorrow because somebody quits, a system goes down, or a hacker decides it's your turn to be their next target.

This means it's not tomorrow when you discover a control isn't working as it should be, but 12 months later. Think of that. In a worst-case scenario where an audit is done on June 20th only for something to change on June 21st, which doesn't get picked up until June 20th the following year. Your entire system has been degrading since Day One unnoticed, leaving you at risk and of being non-compliant for 364 days.

That would be a real blow if you had just spent an entire month of gut-busting effort, as many security professionals do, preparing for the audit because of its perceived importance. After that, it's 11-plus months of comparative relaxation before we embark on the whole frantic process once more.

Managing the audit has become an end in itself when the focus should be on keeping an organization safe. This is like being at a school where all the focus is on studying to pass a test rather than becoming better educated.

The Solution

Wouldn't it be that much better if you 'were on it' the whole time? Then you would not have to make this gut-busting effort to prepare for audits. It would be the difference between driving a car and having to violently slam on the brakes and wrench the wheel around to avoid hitting a wall and never getting near that wall in the first place because you were continually adjusting how you drove. I know which way of driving I'd choose if I wanted to be safer and less stressed.

If we aim to capture evidence proving security controls and compliance measures are operating effectively, then the optimal time to capture and store the evidence that confirms an information security task has been completed is when it is done.

The DIY Option

1. Implement an If-This-Then-That (IFTT) structure that performs an action when evidence documents are uploaded to the correct location.

2. Use a tool like Zapier to automate evidence updates from external tools such as AV, SIEM, or Firewalls to remove the burden of control owners further.

3. Set up an automatically updating dashboard with changes to your risk and compliance measures, so you don't have to spend time and effort manually parsing through evidence uploads and metrics.

The Rivial Platform Approach

That's why we designed the Rivial Platform so that rather than just providing a security 'snapshot' that could effectively be worthless tomorrow, the platform continually monitors risk and compliance controls. So, you have an 'always on' picture of how your controls are operating.

Having that ability relieves you of monumental effort. And, as is often said, consistency — little and often — is much better than infrequent big efforts.

The Rivial platform enables you to do this by providing an ongoing means to integrate uploaded evidence — from multiple manual and automated internal and external sources -- into your Risk and Compliance functions. If evidence is weak or absent, the supported risk and compliance controls will be downgraded in real-time rather than after your next annual IT audit or risk assessment.

When risk and compliance controls are modified, the resulting risk measures and compliance status also change. If these end up outside an organization's risk tolerance levels, an automated alert can be sent to the risk owner for an appropriate response.

Principle 4
Meaningful Metrics & Reports

The Problem

I've already touched on the importance of good communication between those responsible for cybersecurity and an organization's decision-makers.

If the executive management team is to create a culture and organizational structure that helps eradicate risk, they must understand such things as mitigation plans, internal controls, critical processes, and the implications of every security action.

This means that as a CISO or vCISO, you need to be able to communicate your understanding of risk and compliance to the Board of Directors in their own language, using business and financial terms that help them make informed decisions.

Unfortunately, all too often there's a misalignment of language that leads to anything but understanding. Let's take something like risk as an example.

When cybersecurity professionals report to the Board they often talk about the risk status of potential threats and events, categorizing them as high, medium or low risk.

A high-priority risk might be something like a zero-day or ransomware attack that would immediately hit the business. A low-risk item on the other hand may be neither likely nor particularly threatening. Such as credential stuffing on an offline CA server. While an ex-employee walking out with a thumb drive containing a database of your clients would be a medium risk that would fall in between.

All this sounds sensible and logical on the face of it until you ask what these labels actually mean to a business in terms of their cost to an organization if they actually occurred.

So, while we assume an item labelled 'high risk' is more 'dangerous' than something 'low risk', how much and in what way is it riskier?

It's this kind of question business leaders need answering. Unfortunately, that rarely happens which means they aren't equipped with the information required to make the best and most rational decisions possible.

The Solution

Of course, trying to predict uncertain outcomes in the future is difficult but that doesn't mean we shouldn't stick with simple ordinal scales that have no underlying meaning.

For instance, if we use actual industry probabilities from real-life data breaches and then run the numbers through a Monte Carlo analysis, you can get a reasonably clear picture of what might happen. And that can be conveyed in a way that is more easily understood and appreciated by directors who may not be that technically minded.

It's only by taking real numbers and putting them in a business context we can help business leaders understand cybersecurity spending in terms of what will give them the best return on investment and how much risk they are willing to stand.

If we can start to talk more from the perspective of business rather than technology, we can get to a point where we are saying to the Board: "if you spend $10,000 here, we can reduce the risk attached to this system from $200,000 down to just $20,000", then we are getting somewhere.

This is the language that business leaders want to hear and cybersecurity professionals need to speak.

The DIY Option

1. Read "How to Measure Anything in Cybersecurity Risk" by Douglas W. Hubbard & Richard Seiersen.

2. Adopt the spreadsheet provided in the book.

3. Use Rivial's free template to create executive reports.

https://www.rivialsecurity.com/board-report-template. I devised this template several years ago after seeing so many cybersecurity professionals struggle to do this, and it's received great feedback ever since from clients and auditors alike.

The Rivial Platform Approach

At Rivial we are constantly stress-testing our thinking and innovating because we believe this is the way to ensure our CISO clients and MSP partners get the best value from us.

It has helped us develop the advanced security techniques central to our Cybersecurrity Risk Assessment solution that streamlines the process of collecting risk information and improve the risk assessment results in ways that significantly reduce the effort required by our platform users.

These efficiencies also fold perfectly into three tenets of meaningful measures and reports: loss tolerance, cyber risk quantification, and business-friendly reports.

By using the Rivial Platform, organizations have a means to define, in specific financial terms, a loss tolerance curve. Individual information systems that have been risk assessed, can be compared to the loss tolerance curve. The direct financial comparison provides an easy-to-understand visual of each system being below (good) or above (bad) the loss tolerance curve, making risk management decisions easier.

Organizations can customize their loss tolerance curve to meet a specific risk appetite and then 'financially describe' inherent and residual risk in a way that enables the executive management team to make better decisions based on specific, measurable financial KPIs and metrics. The financial risk measures are produced by advanced statistical analysis.

This process is embedded within the Rivial Platform, making ongoing cyber risk quantification much easier and more streamlined. The risk assessment results and all other functions in the platform that make up the cybersecurity program are neatly packaged in an executive-level report.

Principle 5
Integrate and Automate
Everything

The Problem

There is a lot to do in cybersecurity management. A lot of moving pieces and parts that all come together in one holistic program. When we look at other aspects of life in general, from buying movie tickets to grocery shopping, technology is used to make tedious activities simpler and faster through automation, so humans can spend more time being human.

In an industry like cybersecurity, automation is already in use. On what I call the technical 'side' of our industry Security Orchestration, Automation, and Response (SOAR) and similar concepts make full use of automation. The technical folks grew SOAR out of necessity and began maturing predecessor technologies like SEM and SIEM over a decade ago.

But the management side of the cybersecurity industry is only now starting to catch on. In some organizations, covering all the bases could mean having to go to 15 or 20 different locations across multiple systems and chasing maybe 40 or 50 co-workers who might be sitting on the information you need to complete a report. That takes a lot of time and effort you are going to need to repeat month in, month out.

The Solution

It would be much better if you could find ways to automate as many elements as possible. Some software lets you do this OK and other apps don't do this so well and, in any event, you've still got the problem of having to do this for each of them.

The DIY Option

1. The steps to integrate and automate everything overlaps with Principle 3 above.

2. Create an If-This-Then-That (IFTT) structure that automatically performs tedious governance, risk, and compliance tasks.

3. Use tools like Zapier to automate data pulls from external tools like AV, SIEM, Firewalls, etc.

4. Set up your dashboard to automatically update risk and compliance measures. This avoids the time and effort of manually parsing through evidence uploads and metrics.

The Rivial Platform Approach

The Rivial Platform, on the other hand, can take on collection, collation, and processing duties across many apps. Just point it in the right direction, and very soon, you can have the single, comprehensive report you need to present to stakeholders with minimal loss of time or effort.

The platform has a 'point-clicky' integration and automation builder for users to dynamically connect external tools. It's highly customizable, so once set up, it can seamlessly automate all those tedious duties across different cybersecurity management functions that would otherwise have to be done manually. Then, at the end of it, all it takes is one click to generate the report that would previously have taken several days to produce.

For CISOs, vCISOs, MSPs, and anyone with a strategic role who is overburdened with tedious tasks and mired in day-to-day tactical work, this makes the Rivial Platform a huge time saver that enables you to get your head out of the weeds to focus on what is important — properly communicating and collaborating with businesspeople.

An Information Security Director at a financial institution who uses the Rivial Platform has been able to save three or four full days each month updating her risk register so she could be ready to report to the Board. She is now just spending a few minutes on the task because the platform does everything for her automatically.

5
A Final Thought

As we're ending, this is a good point to reprise what I see as the main issues affecting the security industry, not least of which is the growing risk of attack.

There is no escaping the fact that every sector is now facing a tsunami of cyber threats and regulations like never before and that this huge wave will only get bigger as organized criminals, in particular, start to exploit AI. This, combined with an ever-expanding attack surface brought about by growth in the use of IIoT and blockchain technologies, will expose organizations and their data to much greater risk.

And as I've pointed out, our ability as an industry to successfully respond to this threat is being diminished by a shortage of talented professionals who can counter their efforts.

This confluence of growing threats and too few defenders feeds into a perfect storm. This places our industry at a major inflection point, something that is not fully recognized.

And yet, cyberattacks are of potentially monumental significance. You could think of where we are now as equivalent to the 'tobacco years' of the 1950s and '60s when cigarettes' damage to the human body wasn't widely known.

But as it stands, cybersecurity is still too often treated as a tactical cost center rather than something of major strategic importance. Cybersecurity deserves its seat at the big table. However, that will not happen while organizations remain focused on checklists and compliance.

To address this imbalance, the only way is to broaden our use of technology. Just as criminals will use artificial intelligence to up their game, we need to continually think about ways to use software to make cybersecurity management easier. We continue working toward that with the Rivial Platform, an already highly effective tool and one we are constantly developing.

A computer system can certainly decide the best security controls for an organization. Analyzing the relationships between simulated risks, real-world threats, and common security controls is well within reach of modern technology. The business objectives, data, and cultural dynamics may vary from one organization to another, but the foundational principles and control framework of creating a cybersecurity program remain similar.

So, as the world continues to adopt a more collaborative and proactive security mindset, computer systems will more and more be called upon to help security professionals make the best decisions possible from a big data mountain growing exponentially.

That requires a structured new approach, something we have sought to create with our five principles central to the Rivial Platform — automating tedious tasks frees security leaders to focus on more strategic activities.

Of course, technology can't do everything. Security professionals must play a part by ensuring that what they do is seen as an investment in protection and not just a cost center.

And perhaps we are now seeing signs of change with cybersecurity on top of many CIOs' task lists [11] according to research consultancy Gartner, which also forecasts that worldwide spending on information security and risk management is 11.3% up on the year.

But if this money is to be used wisely, they will have to develop and adopt more effective conceptual approaches to cybersecurity rather than remaining wedded to the traditional compliance-based approach, centered around checklists of what a company should or should not do.

And conveying this truth, as I've said, requires those who speak to the Board to do so in the language of business and not of technology. Our industry has been notoriously bad at this in the past, and this must change.

If you want to take the next step toward better cybersecurity program management by applying some 'Rivial thinking,' visit our website, www.rivialsecurity.com/book-offers where you'll find additional resources that will help.

About Rivial

Founded in 2010, Rivial Data Security helps companies meet even the most demanding of cybersecurity challenges by using our market-leading cybersecurity risk and compliance software solution.

Developed by our cybersecurity team using their deep domain knowledge gained from years of building and maintaining cybersecurity programs for complex organizations, the Rivial Platform is based on the five core principles that I've previously described that together make them both more efficient and effective, and underpin The Rivial Platform.

The Rivial Platform is unique in the way it is specifically designed to remove the operational obstacles that stop organizations from protecting their data most effectively.

Automating many time-consuming cybersecurity functions, enables CISOs and Virtual CISOs to take a highly integrated and efficient approach that's far more effective at managing their cybersecurity resources.

The Rivial Platform enables us to add extreme amounts of value, which is why it's now the world's leading cybersecurity program automation platform, used by all industries and sectors across the world.

And though we never ask our clients to rank us, we have been told on more than one occasion that we are an organization's favorite among all their vendors, not just those in cybersecurity. Considering that most organizations are working with hundreds or thousands of suppliers this is an exceptional endorsement.

I love hearing from clients who tell me they want to get better at managing cybersecurity risk because I know we can help them and this can be a turning point that will send them down a better road. So, when they say to me after a risk assessment meeting: 'that wasn't so bad' that may not sound like much but it's music to my ears.

Endnotes

1   cybercrime damages were put at around $6 trillion

2   cybercrimes are costing the equivalent of about 0.8% of the world's GDP.

3   ransomware attacks on companies were looking to be a third higher

4   http://www3.weforum.org/docs/WEF_Global_Risk_Report_2020.pdf

5   https://cybersecurityventures.com/60-percent-of-small-companies-close-within-6-months-of-being-hacked/

6   https://www.businessinsider.com/warren-buffett-cybersecurity-berkshire-hathaway-meeting-2017-5

7   https://www.youtube.com/watch?v=d_mG_SPzFj0

8   https://www.rivialsecurity.com/it-risk-compliance-management-software

9   https://www.mimecast.com/blog/ransomwares-relentless-rise-strains-security-teams/

10 https://www.mimecast.com/blog/ransomwares-relentless-rise-strains-security-teams/

11 https://www.gartner.com/en/newsroom/press-releases/2022-09-26-gartner-says-cybersecurity-application-and-integration-strategies-and-cloud-are-top-technology-priorities-for-midsize-enterprises

Made in United States
Troutdale, OR
05/03/2024

19610242R00037